VIOLIN 2

More Folk Strings

For String Quartet or String Orchestra

Arranged and Edited by Joanne Martin

Cover Design: Candy Woolley
Illustrations: Rama Hughes

© 2003 Summy-Birchard Music
division of Summy-Birchard Inc.
Exclusive print rights administered by
Alfred Music Publishing, Co., Inc.
All Rights Reserved

ISBN-10: 1-58951-161-1
ISBN-13: 978-1-58951-161-3

Any duplication, adaptation or arrangement of the compositions contained in this collection requires the written consent of the Publisher.
No part of this book may be photocopied or reproduced in any way without permission. Unauthorized uses are an infringement of the U.S. Copyright Act and are punishable by law.

INTRODUCTION

More Folk Strings is a collection of folk melodies from around the world arranged for strings. Some of these tunes were part of my childhood, and I have many happy memories of the hours spent singing them with my mother while she played the piano. Others are melodies I discovered more recently and are included because I enjoy playing them.

Unlike classical music, which normally has an "authentic" version, folk music often exists in many versions, with differences in the melody or lyrics. Sometimes several countries lay claim to a melody because a group of people moved to a new country and took their music with them. Most folk songs were sung and played for many years before they were written down, and their original composer is usually unknown. This collection includes melodies in a variety of moods and with rhythmic patterns that are representative of their country of origin.

The arrangements in *More Folk Strings* can be effective with players at a variety of levels. Less experienced players can play the melody line, learning it partly by ear and partly by reading. Some pieces in the collection are easier than others, and teachers can choose which are appropriate for their particular group. In order to provide maximum flexibility, the collection is available in a number of instrumentations, which are the same as those used in *Festive Strings* and *More Festive Strings*:

    More Folk Strings for String Quartet or Orchestra

    More Folk Strings for Violin Ensemble
    More Folk Strings for Viola Ensemble
    More Folk Strings for Cello Ensemble
        For two, three, or four violin, viola, or cello players in any combination of these instruments

    More Folk Strings for Solo Violin
    More Folk Strings for Solo Viola
    More Folk Strings for Solo Cello
        For use with: *More Folk Strings for String Quartet or Orchestra*
            or   *More Folk Strings for Violin, Viola,* or *Cello Ensemble*
            or   *More Folk Strings Piano Accompaniments*

    More Folk Strings Piano Accompaniments
        For use with: *More Folk Strings for String Quartet or Orchestra*
            or   *More Folk Strings for Violin, Viola,* or *Cello Ensemble*
            or   *More Folk Strings for Solo Violin, Viola,* or *Cello*

The arrangements are in keys chosen to be accessible and resonant. Shifting has been kept to a minimum, and where a shift is required, finger numbers indicate the first note in a new position. A fingering in parentheses means to remain in the same position.

In *More Folk Strings for String Quartet or Orchestra,* the melody is passed around so that all members of the ensemble can have the opportunity to play the tune. Score and parts are marked with "Melody" and "Harmony" to help players bring out the melody at the appropriate moment. These orchestra arrangements can be played by a string quartet, since the instrumentation is complete without the bass part. Most of the time, Violin 3 duplicates the Viola part; where the parts are different, the Violin 3 part appears in small notes in the score.

Both rehearsal letters and measure numbers are provided. In the orchestra arrangements some of the pieces have rehearsal letters A1, A2, B1, and so on. These markings need explanation only if a group uses the String Quartet or Orchestra parts together with the Solo parts or with the Piano Accompaniment. The String Quartet or Orchestra parts have the repeats written out, with the melody in a different voice the second time. In these pieces, A1 in the Orchestra part matches letter A for the first time in the Solo part, A2 matches A for the second time, and so on.

During the preparation of this project, I have imposed on the good nature of numerous friends, colleagues, students, and family members. They gave their time generously to play the pieces, and their suggestions were invaluable in the revision process. In particular I thank Karen Barg Camacho, Milan Durecek, Mary Helen Law, Carolyn McCall, Ivan Pokus, Carole Pollard, Judi Price-Rosen, Patricia Shand, Fiona Shand, Ellen Shertzer, Carole Shoaf, Ruth Wiwchar, the "crusty academics," Karin Erhardt, who provided the cello fingerings, and Karla Philipp, who did the bass fingerings and as usual provided a wealth of helpful advice.

Especially, I acknowledge my daughter Shauna for her continually cheerful encouragement and my husband Peter for being, as always, incredibly patient and caring, even when asked to play yet one more draft version or to proofread one more folder of parts. Their support gave me the energy to complete this project.

More Folk Strings is dedicated to the memory of my niece Alison, whose brief years were so full of music, dance, and the joy of life.

Enjoy!

                                                                                            Joanne Martin

Contents

Introduction 2

Shoo Fly 4

Tancuj, Tancuj 6

Linstead Market 8

Un canadien errant 9

Bella Bimba 10

The Leaving of Liverpool 10

I've Been Working on the Railroad 12

Auprès de ma blonde 13

Sakura 14

Good Evening 16

Teachers' Notes 17

* See Introduction for explanation of rehearsal letters

TANCUJ, TANCUJ

Violin 2

Slovakia
Arranged by JOANNE MARTIN

* See Introduction for explanation of rehearsal letters

UN CANADIEN ERRANT

Violin 2

Canada
Arranged by JOANNE MARTIN

BELLA BIMBA

Violin 2

Italy
Arranged by JOANNE MARTIN

THE LEAVING OF LIVERPOOL

England
Arranged by JOANNE MARTIN

The Leaving of Liverpool - 2

I'VE BEEN WORKING ON THE RAILROAD

Violin 2

United States
Arranged by JOANNE MARTIN

AUPRÈS DE MA BLONDE

Violin 2

Canada
Arranged by JOANNE MARTIN

SAKURA

Violin 2

Japan
Arranged by JOANNE MARTIN

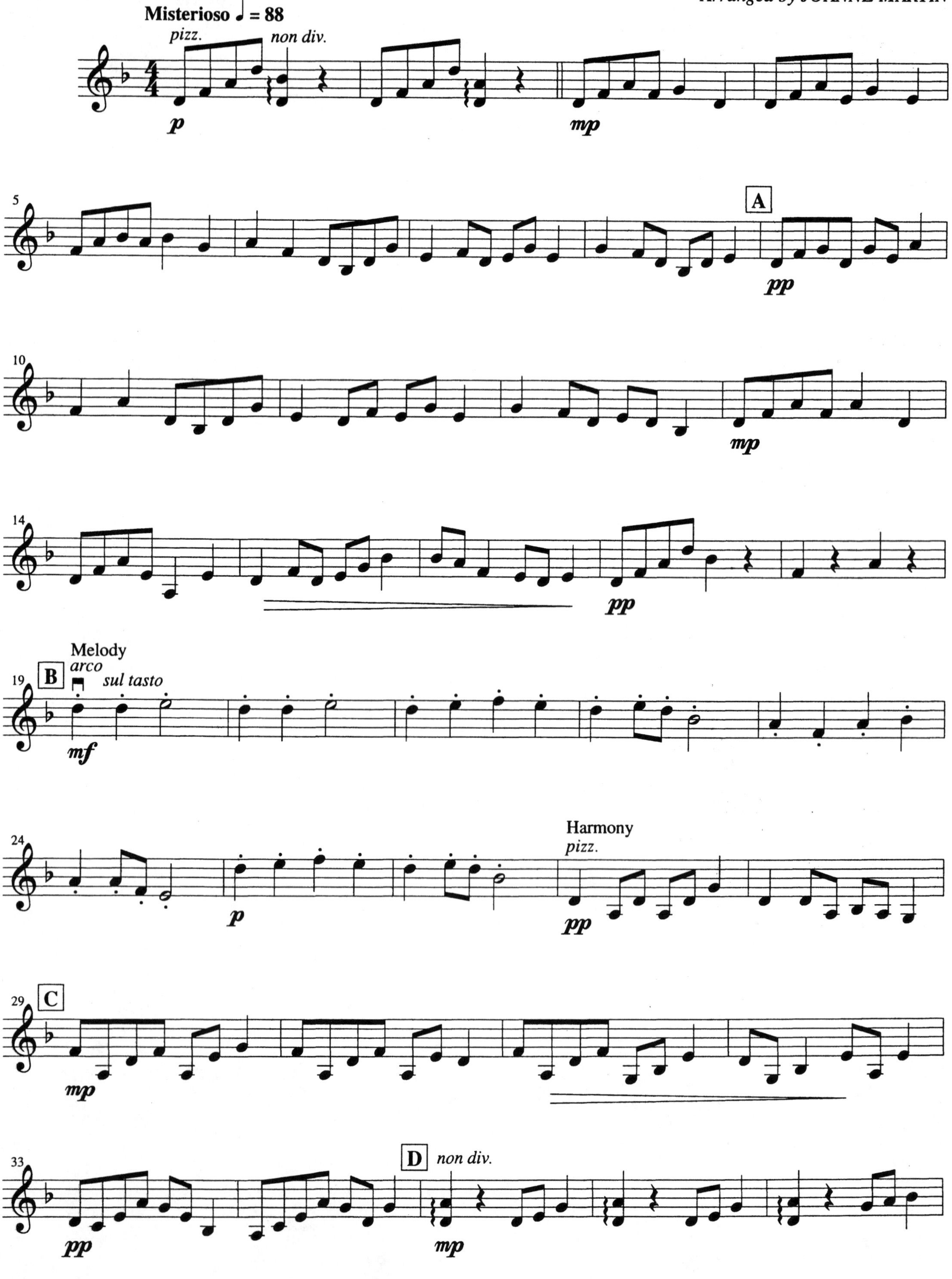

TEACHERS' NOTES

SHOO FLY - United States

> Shoo fly, don't bother me, *(repeat 3 times)*
> For I belong to somebody.
>
> I feel, I feel, I feel like a morning star, *(repeat)*
> Shoo fly, don't bother me...
>
> I feel, I feel, I feel like a singing bird, *(repeat)*
> Shoo fly, don't bother me...
>
> I feel, I feel, I feel like a bubbling brook, *(repeat)*
> Shoo fly, don't bother me...

"Shoo Fly" is a well-known folk tune from the southern United States that has been popular since the nineteenth century. During the Civil War, soldiers sang it with the lyrics "Shoo fly, don't bother me 'cause I belong to Company G."

This arrangement imitates the traditional fiddling style. The melody should be played with slightly staccato bow strokes. The eighth-note countermelodies in the accompaniment parts should be played with open strings wherever possible and a *legato* on-the-string bow stroke.

TANCUJ, TANCUJ - Slovakia

> Tancuj, tancuj, vykrúcaj, vykrúcaj,
> Len mi pecku nezrúcaj, nezrúcaj!
> Dobrá pecka na zimu, na zimu,
> Nemá každý perinu, perinu.
> Tra la la la tra la la la
> La la la la la la la la la la

Tancuj (pronounced "tan-tzui") means dance. This exuberant song is from the Slovácko region in the northwest of Slovakia near the Czech Republic and is probably the best known of the Slovak folk tunes. The first stanza describes dancing around a wood stove, but the dancers are cautioned not to knock over the stove because winter is coming. Other stanzas describe a soldier, a gypsy woman, and her magic spells.

This arrangement should be played energetically with a lively tempo and joyous mood, and the syncopations in the melody should be brought out. The accompaniment parts should be light and staccato, off the string if possible.

LINSTEAD MARKET - Jamaica

> Carry mi ackee go a Linstead Market
> Not a quatty worth sell. *(repeat these lines)*
>
> O, Lord, what a night, not a bite,
> What a Saturday night! *(repeat)*
>
> Everybody come feel up, feel up
> Not a quatty worth sell. *(repeat)*

"Linstead Market" is a Jamaican calypso song. The calypso originated during the time of slavery, when slaves were forbidden to speak to each other, but rhythmic singing was allowed since it was thought to make work more efficient. An *ackee* is a Jamaican vegetable, and a *quatty* is a coin worth about a penny.

The syncopated calypso rhythm is easier to feel than to read. It may be helpful to sing the melody or to play groups of eighth notes, accenting the fourth and seventh eighth notes (**1** 2 3 - **1** 2 3 - **1** 2) before reading the music on the page.

UN CANADIEN ERRANT - Canada

> Un canadien errant, banni de ses foyers, *(repeat)*
> Parcourait en pleurant des pays étrangers. *(repeat)*
>
> Un jour, triste et pensif, assis au bord des flots, *(repeat)*
> Au courant fugitif il adressa ces mots: *(repeat)*
>
> "Si tu vois mon pays, mon pays malheureux, *(repeat)*
> Va, dis à mes amis que je me souviens d'eux." *(repeat)*

"Un canadien errant" (translated as "a wandering Canadian") is the song of a young man who sits by a stream flowing north to Canada and asks the water to tell his friends how much he misses them and his homeland. After the rebellion of 1837, many Canadians escaped punishment by fleeing to the United States. These lyrics were likely written around 1840 by one of the exiles and set to an old French tune. Some versions of this song contain four-bar phrases, with the melody note in the third bar held for two bars. I have used three-bar phrases, as in the original French melody.

In keeping with the nostalgic melancholy of the lyrics, this arrangement can be played quite freely, but it is important to keep the tempo moving. Players should feel the phrases in three-bar groupings, with one beat to a bar.

BELLA BIMBA - Italy

Ma come balli bella bimba, bella bimba, bella bimba
Ma come balli bella bimba, come balli, balli ben.

Guarda che passa, la villanella
Agilee snella, sa ben ballar.
Ma come balli bella bimba…

Danza al mattina, danza alla.
Sera, sempre leggera, sembra volar.
Ma come balli bella bimba…

"Bella Bimba" (which means "beautiful girl") is an Italian folk song set to a Triestine folk tune. The lyrics describe the girl's beauty and how gracefully she dances.

This song is light and joyous. In the accompaniment the quarter notes on the second and third beats of the bar should be quite detached and light. The section at letter B should be more legato than the first section. In bars 21 and 37, the melody stops on the first beat and the accompanying parts play a change of harmony on beat 2. All parts play on beat 3, which is the pickup to the chorus.

THE LEAVING OF LIVERPOOL - England

Farewell to Prince's Landing Stage
River Mersey, fare thee well.
I am bound for California
A place I know right well.

So fare thee well, my own true love,
When I return united we will be.
It's not the leaving of Liverpool that grieves me
But my darling when I think of thee.

I'm bound off for California
By the way of stormy Cape Horn,
And I'm bound to write you a letter, love,
When I am homeward bound.
So fare thee well…

Liverpool is a seaport on the northwest coast of England. "The Leaving of Liverpool" dates from the latter half of the nineteenth century, and the lyrics express a young sailor's regret as he departs on a merchant clipper ship bound for California. Although the song originated in England, it is so popular in Ireland that it is frequently considered part of the Irish folk tradition.

In this arrangement it is important to keep the harmony parts moving, but always less prominent than the melody. The harmony parts imitate the perpetual swell of the sea.

I'VE BEEN WORKING ON THE RAILROAD - United States

I've been workin' on the railroad, all the live long day.
I've been workin' on the railroad, just to pass the time away.
Don't you hear the whistle blowing? Rise up so early in the morn.
Don't you hear the captain shouting, "Dinah, blow your horn?"

Dinah, won't you blow, Dinah, won't you blow,
Dinah, won't you blow your horn? *(repeat these lines)*

Someone's in the kitchen with Dinah, someone's in the kitchen, I know.
Someone's in the kitchen with Dinah, strumming on the old banjo and singing,
Fee, fie, fiddle-e-i-o, fee, fie, fiddle-e-i-o-o-o-o.
Fee, fie, fiddle-e-i-o, strumming on the old banjo.

"I've Been Working on the Railroad" is a well-known campfire song from the United States. Some versions of this song include only the sections at letter A and B, and some songbooks have the section from letter C to the end ("Dinah won't you blow…") as a separate song.

The train whistle sounds, such as in bars 2 and 4, can be accented and raucous. Throughout this arrangement, the dotted rhythms should be played as triplets. The chug-a-chug figure (two eighth notes followed by a quarter note) should be merely a rhythmic background to the melody and countermelody. The chromaticisms in the harmony parts should be brought out. At bar 42, all parts pause on a half note except the viola, which has moving notes in the last half of the bar.

AUPRÈS DE MA BLONDE - Canada

Au jardin de mon père, les lilas sont fleuris, *(repeat)*
Tous les oiseaux du monde vienn'nt y faire leurs nids.

Auprès de ma blonde, il fait bon, fait bon, fait bon
Auprès de ma blonde, il fait bon dormir.

La caill', la tourterelle, et la jolie perdrix, *(repeat)*
Et ma blanche colombe, qui chante jour et nuit.
Auprès de ma blonde...

Ell' chante pour les filles qui n'ont pas de mari, *(repeat)*
Pour moi ne chante guère car j'en ai un joli.
Auprès de ma blonde...

"Auprès de ma blonde" is a French-Canadian folk song based on a nineteenth-century melody from France. Originally a military marching song, it is now a popular children's song. The title means "near my sweetheart." The singer hears all the birds singing in her father's garden and thinks about how much she misses her husband, who has been captured by the Dutch army.

This piece should be played lightly, keeping the tempo moving. Off-the-string bowing in the accompaniment parts will help keep the texture light. In bars 48 and 49 the rhythm of the melody is altered to emphasize the conclusion.

SAKURA - Japan

Sakura, sakura
Yayoi no sora wa
Miwatasu kagiri
Kasumi ka kumoka
Nioi zo izuru
Iza ya, iza ya,
Mini yukan

The title of this well-known Japanese folk song means "cherry blossom." The lyrics describe the beauty of the flowers and the joy they bring in springtime. The melody is based on the pentatonic minor scale, which is typical of many traditional Japanese songs.

The pizzicato accompaniment imitates the sound of the koto, the Japanese 13-stringed instrument similar to the zither. The grace notes in the pizzicato accompaniment, such as in bar 20, should be played with a single pizzicato stroke, pulling the string slightly sideways with the left hand as the finger lifts. Pizzicato double-stops should be rolled slightly and played *non-divisi*. The melody should be played with a detached stroke, *sul tasto*, to create a mysterious and exotic sound.

GOOD EVENING - Denmark

God Aften, God Aften, jeg byder Jer Singgot. *(repeat)*
God Aften min Mutter, god Aften min Fatter
God Aften min Pige, her har du mig atter,
Og straeb saa, og straeb sa, at vi kan faa in Vals.
Og hør du lille Pige vil du valse med mig,
Valse med mig, valse mid mig,
Og hør du lille Pige vil du valse med mig,
Valse med mig en Valse.

"Good Evening" is a dance tune from Jutland, which is the mainland portion of Denmark. The lyrics are in the form of a conversation between a young man and the young woman he fancies and invites to dance a waltz.

The basic pulse remains the same throughout the piece, and the first beat in each bar should be strong, regardless of the meter. At letters C and F, the dotted half note in the new tempo equals the half note in the previous section. The inner voices should be kept very light, with eighth notes slightly off the string.